When the Wood is Green

When the Wood is Green

POEMS

Paul McCann

Slough Press

College Station, Texas

Thanks the following journals for publishing many of these earlier poems: *Hawaii Pacific Review, Argestes, Fickle Muses, Bayou Magazine, Berkeley Poetry Review,* and National Poetry Competition Winners: The Chester H. Jones Foundation.

Cover Art: Chuck Taylor
Book Design: Buffalo Times Productions

For orders and information:

Slough Press
3009 Normand
College Station, Texas 77845
sloughpress@gmail.com
www.sloughpressbooks.com

Library of Congress Cataloging-in-Publication Data

McCann, Paul, 1982-
[Poems Selections]
When the wood is green : poems / Paul McCann.
   pages cm
ISBN 978-0-941720-78-6 (pbk. : alk. paper)
I. Title.
PS3613.C34547A6 2014
813'.6--dc23
                    2014012819

To my wife and soul mate, Tolly.

Contents

When the Wood is Green

Shadowboxing the Sunrise

If these things should be done to us when the wood is green, what will happen when it is dry?

—Luke 23: 30-31

Coconut Champagne

The unpracticed symphony of youth
begins to take shape of itself
where no one can hear
smiles are exchanged… yes…
and finally sadness.

She says the bigger kids have cars
but it's easier in the open.
Either way damned awkward
but on the upbeats
crescendo bringing with it
waves of secrecy
this only is not hollow
though we strike the world as a timpani
and end as names on a bathroom wall.

If you follow the lines of sheet music
like a puzzle you will
come closer to understanding
the madness of it.

Notes dart backwards
from the bugle horn
penetrate the arbitrary
and mock the saxophone
bending up to touch its fingers.

Life layers itself and the melody
more transparent now yields to
the complexity of support.

Bottomless is the chorus
speaking Greek does not reach
the crowd.

Not here.

So many vapors
carried away by the wind
ask for possibility and
find a boy
hinting towards manhood
still not knowing what it sounds like.

Grammar School Valentine

They are bringing me gifts
for the practice
    of the ritual
            of love-making
that we know not of beyond this
    simple civics lesson
for grammar school paramours.

The chalky hearts relate indifferent desires
You're Special, Cool Cat, Be My Valentine,
            The rare I Love You.

It is necessary to use few words.
    These hearts are too small
to contain much more,

but know instinctively
they are meant to be consumed.

    Hallmark sentiments discarded before dodgeball.

The more courteous lovers
bring home these trinkets of love
before they are abandoned
    and some, I've heard at least,
keep them locked away for years
in shoe boxes.

The wiser teacher stands before us
To give her sermon…
she's divorced (and mother says *the husband just took off*)

"Children, all that you are given today
will be taken away tomorrow,
even those relics of love you did not know
you possessed. Taste them now."

But we just keep counting
to see who has more.
I stole Frank's.
He is, after all, diabetic.

The Ontological Boss

Between cups of coffee
and the obligatory breakfast bagel
bought by the dozens
in the aisles of a management memo,
between the Strategic Assessment Report,
    and the presentation on Executive Diagnosis of Value,
recite the ontological argument.

Say it like grace.

Or perhaps,

Reside by the comfort glow.
There's something you must see.
This half hour oblivion measures
your life:
The miracle cure?
St. John's Wort and cabbage soup.
A new apartment, a better neighborhood,
talking with a salesman's grace.
Yes. Yes. Yes. Yes
and this too as
the commercial fog rolls
beneath November skies and
envelops the commodity of souls.
That Being of which none greater
can be conceived.
Existence here is better
than existence there.
Your boss exists.

The Henchman's Legacy

So little Molly Brown
from the suburbs can shop safe again
and the narcotic streets swept clean
by vagabond soles
are free to neon twilight.

And yet,
my body aches
with some strange itch
for those Gotham nights.

Joker tickling the crowd's
blessed misery
with the one about the paraplegic prostitute
    and the one legged John
B-low me down.
and Riddler smoked
so much hashish
he stumped himself.

Paper chasing the empty streets
like tumbleweeds of the American Dream
we ran,
knowing they were far worse
than laughing gas bombs, even.
A dream is some strange vampire
that preys upon the blood of the ordinary.

We Kings of Refuse.
We Princes of the Vacant—
              Maniacal cackling.

No catch phrases in conversations
of profound parody.
My words were omitted
from the skyline drama

because they could not be contained
within the dialogue bubble.

We patriots of vagrant vigilantes
    fighting out freedom when

P-WIFF!!! CRASH!!!! Z-RACK!!! BAM!!!
    And goddamn.

Now only residue Starbuck mornings
    all helpless and beholden
to some "hero"
who decorates his name with a phallus.

But look closely behind the register
at Orange Julius.
The clerk has a wide smile
thinking of some outside joke
looking to be inside again,
notes the pale and careless hands
of the merchant's new oblivion,
and wonders what strange treasures
they will again discard.

Hubris

A vague recollection
of some forgotten mediocrity
revealed in the momentary imbalance
of schoolyard shame
meant to engender humility
toward the gnashing of teeth
of childhood strangers.

Only in your imagination
may you stand up in the playground Bermuda
--a casualty of indifference.
Trouble passed over
in favor of some anecdotal civility
regarding Carson or Foucault.

Only later do you
realize you were the casualty
of their cowardice.
They would not suffer the insult
but these useless clouds,
these branches of dying flesh
demand it of you.

Humility is for a priest,
anger for a man,
pride for a god.

So some secret strength
is nursed
from the imaginary to the real.

Carried forward into a more distant spring,
this Olympian strolls
the schoolyard of this Earth
thermos in hand
waiting for the next game of tag.

John Updike

I discovered you in college
    in the anxious eighties of me,
(you drew with such definition
those fuzzy borders)
kicking around in the back
of a dorm room closet,
still the reluctant hostage of youth.

And it wasn't completely without guilt
    that we embraced.

Your God did not stand with the same vigor
as your shame.

We met again in the nineties.
    The familiarity of your WASPy New England
I apologetically defended.
        You, gorgeous martini of the suburbs.
    You, beautiful time capsule of Elementary America
        in crayola wandering.

So many Others pushing past you
    could not help but pause in your world
    awed at the drama of your dentist appointments,
your tinfoil ducks.

But deferential, you could take notes on a New America
    though its edges rubbed so brusquely
on your sixties and seventies. You learned with sadness
silk pajamas are cliché
All roads merge at gunpowder streets

And with twenty years of borrowed relevance…
    Yes, still…

The fashions of your improbable God.

Lacan's Autonomous Ego

Is what thinks in my place, then, another I?
--Jacques Lacan

The heat of that August night
was moist hyperbole
into which he stumbled Prufrock-like
with a nausea fueled by beer
and a pierced
solipsism
that made him contemptuous of
the allusion's impotence.

So that, in faded and torn Khaki pants,
his hurried gait through streetlamp inquisitions
seemed a sort of skydiving.
The evening's grudge had shattered him
and those broken pieces coalesced
around only known desires.

I do not know the aggregate man
who emerged in the parking lot.
Only that it was your rubbery throat
that seemed to yield willingly
to the metal of his blade
and not a tire.

Punctured, the air escapes and scitters
in crisp whispers through the humid emptiness.
One pathetic, unforgiving stab
at a decentered garage.
S/s/S/s/S/s/S/s/S/s!!!
Walking away, what was to you
the night's muted exclamation point was
for him,
A chorus of Angels.

A Homeless Poem for Lovers

You said it began
    with a promise
long ago after a stolen kiss.
Our company was disapproving
    certain we were shagging
in some shadowy corner of the town
    and why not?
Many lovers do.
Their sex smells like wet oak.
Whispering: This will happen in time.

In time…
    In time…
        In time I thought

I would die not from a loss of blood
    but of tears
        expelled in rivulets.

That frame in which you've placed us
will not do…
the canvas is too big.
The field dwarfs the two naked figures
Stumbling blindly for its center.

Instead, border us with curses, shouting, a vacancy.

I washed ashore in Freeport, remember?
My face smooth like a seal.
    Too broken to speak.
I was the ocean. I was the sand.
I was the Sea King
    because I was nothing else.
So silent in the sand
    The ocean whispers for me…
        I love you

but I'm not here
I laugh with you
but I'm not here.

The prodigal son is supposed to return
to a feast not this shit.
Go away. Go away. Go away
    and become a stranger.
I will not go back there...
    cold weather, a cold people aspiring to numbness
You're a spoiled brat!
Good. I will be young then
    And the pain of youth is infinitely more noble
than the toil of adulthood.
I cannot go but I cannot stay
nor will not
nor going nor staying

When I was here/there, it snowed and sweated all the time
    and we lived in constant fear of the suncloud.
They said I could stay but I had to go
    but here I can go but I have to stay.
I will inhabit the fertile lands of Staygo
    (Darling, you've already had it decorated and it's beauti-
ful.)
    The Sea King will claim it with his uncertain Queen.

You're a pathetic fool
to demand something of the wind
The Ancient Greeks would see the false pride.
O' if you were an ancient Greek
you'd be a fairy tale.

My heart is an anchor that I no longer have the strength to
lift.

I will gather seaweed and make a joke of it.
            Though some guests will still be offended by the
ritual's power.

Be careful. The beach is a temporary place...
Sharks wait greedily past the first sand bar.

A riptide can carry you off to sea.
A fisherman's hook might be buried in the driftwood.
Sand mites burrow into your flesh to lay their eggs.

But know that what we plant here washes away
so that it may gain some permanence farther ashore.

I will surround you with beauty.

The sand mites chitter and dorsal fins dance in the moon-
light.

Marco and the Game

Marco and the game begins
Eyes closed
And still a blur of light.
Regret smells like chlorine.
Marco, a false smile edged
with wrinkles and she
touches the back of her leg
to itch and look away
on the crest of a hill
horizon beneath her.
He thinks
of what it means to be big.
Marco and photographs are discarded
and disappear
somewhere in the squishy corners
of the infinite pool
that joyfully drowns us.
Concerned and compassionate eyes of a man.
The baby in his arms is very symbolic.
Marco and parting more difficult
than the journey from the womb.
the ripples expanding outward
will not beach.
She would have been six today!
Polo! Polo! Polo!
And this is the world
baptized with a hard slap.
Tagged.
The crowd jeers.
You're it! You're it! You're it!

Life in Tributary

In the mountain, there is a river;
deep and slow-moving
replenished yearly by the bleeding
of the snow melt.
In its icy afterbirth,
your body will diminish by degrees
and drift like the pine needles.

In the hills, there is a river;
deep and slow-moving
upon which you might raft
(back to beech bark)
gazing up at the thin branches
that criss-cross above you
like the hands of an infant
at prayer.

In the valley, there is a river;
deep and slow-moving
where you might float
in the shallow rapids of adolescence
past the older men
in catfish exile
cautiously stabbing your currents.

In the coastal plains, there is a river;
deep and slow-moving
where you hover helplessly
in the tepid waters of your own tears
framing the majesty
of the mountains of your youth,
hearing only the impersonal breathing
of the sea.

A Monday Cloud

Dropped headfirst into a pool of coldwater
the self, self-conscious
putters about to a familiar song
front loaded in the fog.

Suffocating in the vacuous sack
of climate controlled interiors,
commuter cars initiate
the helpless strokes to the shore
of a vast humanity,

Selfish,   lazy,
loving,   curious,   self-absorbed
Finding a half-hearted salvation
in a roasted bean.

Stares turned to nods
slighted greetings,
crafted salutes.
Everything after
a protracted negotiation.

Will you be?   I be.
Be   and   seem
skirmish
from distant trenches
mined the enemy's location
in false smiles, a loaded question
before the first great battle
leaves you battered and broken.

Seem welcomes retreat
and again. The evening be more than the day.

A chalky smile dissolves
into that toothless chalice

let slip the knotted tie
and breaks the self with starlight.

Obsolescence

First he grumbled in stuttered sighs
that aborted a pregnant pause
amidst the
blue and grey and mauve flower patches
browned with coffee stains.

Second, he forgot what
he was fighting for
and his lust
turned to dispassionate
rubbing in the
television twilight.

Third, he dropped
his emotions in a bottle,
turned his fruits to pitch,
staggered the moment
to tease the evening sky.

Finally he lost
his sour button smile
in the night
to some great insult
cleverly passed among
rumors of war.

Now he sits
with his knees unstitched
debating the vapors
actions too grand for gesture.

Is he welcome —
this giant
shadowboxing the sunrise?

The Plagiarist

She enters with the confidence
only secrets bring.

A blue denim jacket
tight above the hips hints
a skirt, androgyny
like a Greek.

I respect that she does
not want to impress but
to disappoint. She will deny everything
before it can be denied to her.
A Degree
In Disappointment.
Why else to say:

The author cleverly combines the
elements of a traditional Bildungsroman
with the elements of existentialist philosophy.

A simpler thesis
would have furrowed
an eyebrow,
elicited an exhausted sigh.
She wants to teach
me to see the me she sees,
articulate in disapproval only.

I am with her,
there is never any intimacy
among the impressive and the honorable.
Our negotiation, a subtle sexual posturing
for there can be no learning the lesson
without learning the me
that I cannot give up.

And scented leaves
that began screaming
larceny are all muted
by a careless creasing, fumbled hands
banished to a lavender couch.

She, drowning me in false sobs
                  and curt goodbyes
leaves on the lessoning.

Portrait of the Artist as a Relatively Young Man

We now ask someone to take responsibility
For the death
of the author
of this poem.

Uncle Sam wants you
because any guilt, karma, or vengeance
must be centered on a single individual
who for the sake of the greater good
will vanquish the enemies of the state.
A patriot in a time of patriotic fervor…

Make sure the murder is for selfless reasons.

Trade your heroism for his villainy
since this poem was originally presented
as a product of the state.
A thing even children could look to
with civic pride
knowing they too played their part,
however small, in its creation.

"An intersection of my time and place,"
he said.
"A non-transcendent meditation
of the royal we."

However, several witnesses have come forward
and testified that the author is prone
to bouts of
self-importance,
and that he has fled the stain of human companionship.
Further evidence demonstrates
that he is solely responsible for the poem;

that he wrote it
in a glossy overpriced Moleskin
while feeling sorry for himself.

There he sits,
fighting some unspeakable sickness,
with his legs scissored
wearing an affectatious hat
cuckolding our mockery
with his own impotence.

My Social Contract

The problem, really?
    I suppose
We married too young,
    Me and my America.

I should have been thinking of the future but…
    She looked so hot,
In that white bra and lacey slip,
    leaning over the keg.
I just wanted to fuck her brains out,
    and almost did
when she gave me that highway smile.

I picked her up from behind
    with two tree trunk arms
strong from the hard work of an earlier time.
She seemed game on the dining room table
where I slid off those red, white, and blue panties
    and put them in her purse
which seemed to tremble there
    even when I wasn't moving.

But before the blessed moment,
    right before the act,
I heard other party guests,
    or thought I did.
Some reformed Greenwich hipster
    reciting Ayn Rand
in the idea pantry.

After that, she was more modest.
    I did the honorable thing…
But she was never as hot,
not as that night,
    on the cracked oak of the dinner table,
bread crumbs around her thighs,

her head gently bumping
    The salt and pepper shakers
with each dry heave.

When things inevitably cooled,
    I wanted to fight everyone.

The sanctimonious priests of the AM radio,
    the small town belief bullies
    swinging their words like a thermos,
the bar-fly philistine
    drowning his slack-jawed errors
in a grail of indifference.
Let his New Jersey bouncers send me flying.

And the powerful…
    The pious quarterback
arrogant in golden-haired virtue.
Give me one good hit on the gentle giants.
    The determined Navy SEAL
Cloaking his soul in patriotic discipline.
Violence of my kind has nothing to do with winning
    or fearing.
I want to lose.
My eyes blackened, my liver bruised.
My cracked ribs,
    scraping the nicotine stains of lung tissue.

I didn't want to register my disgust
    In dynamite overcoats,
Or bullet brunches in high school cafeterias.
I wanted to fight the way lovers fight
when they discover the horrible truth
of the other's inevitable mediocrity…
Violently taking back
something of that esteem
    I once so dearly declared,
etched in the rituals of my aching heart
and the tedious boasting of tolerable friends.
That esteem is the province of childhood
and left behind with the greatest reluctance.

Strike and tear and punish
The ocular bone cracked
The upper lip split into a ghoulish and bloody
V

so that you
might come to terms with the disappointment of it.
    forcing the other side into mutual forgiveness
so at the officer's inevitable arrival
 and the registered disgust of his knocking
        at routine reports of domestic violence.

What am I to say?

America hit me first.

No. And how dare he scribble down
My smells and odors,
Catalogue my vices
My country tripped
outside this crappy apartment.
Tripped and fell.
    My country lies there still.

Slipped on a toy plane, I say.
And then another crashed
    into those two fleshy thighs

A Nasty fall that left
some greater thing, still born.

The damn kids and the drinking
and the tile is hard.

And despite all the blood
and my own bruises and scratches,
the broken shin and the swollen wrist,
you have to believe me, officer
I never touched her.

Summer of Punk

I couldn't hear you when I was seventeen
watching beautiful dancers on the football field
showing so much cleavage for the middle brow.
I imagined I could have them
all
    to myself, each inviting.

I would have mocked your dysfunctional concern
    with skater kids
        (burn-out, spoiled, bitchy
        adolescence on the freeway,
        melting).
You rubbed elbows brusquely
    with the vocal apathy of grunge.

So you were just crying, cable-car prophets then
    drifting in the easy breeze of arty San Francisco.
Might as well have been Paris.
My third coast was brown with oil
    and immigrants, and bearded Country.

Instead, we met in my late thirties
    after my first colonoscopy,
You, by your irritated guitar.
    Me, in business casual next to an anxious bass
that echoed the horrors of my silenced majority.
We embraced awkwardly
in cubicles of fluorescent despair,
    burned tie-dye shirts
in payroll lounges and faculty meetings.

Sometimes, I see you in the eyes of another.
    Tech support.
There, in his earpiece, hopefully
    is the buzzing of the high hat
sounding my muted discontent

and the collective sigh
of our generation.

Resurrecting Daniel

I saw Dan at the wake,
which was ironic
because it was his wake
and everyone felt real awkward
when he walked in the kitchen door smoking menthols
in the suede shirt he used to play pool in.
Me, especially, cause I had brought a date
and it was my idea to bury him
in the mausoleum.

It was cheaper, you know,
but someone had rolled the stone away
so to speak.
Is it you? I asked.
Are you a ghost?
I'M ALL HERE! he said
and rolled back those familiar suede sleeves
to reveal the wounds on his wrist.
Still bleeding down the palms of his hands onto the rug
but no one complained… it was his carpet.

Everyone crowded in and felt compelled to touch him
before Brian started the inquiry:
"So what is all this anyway?
Are you the second coming?
Will you usher in the end of the world
and punish the sinners?"

No? Then what?

Simply this:
A manifestation of chaos
whose prophecy is the simple reminder
that the sun may or may not rise tomorrow,
a disorder, an anomaly.

And the mood became particularly somber,
even for a wake.
Let's think this through.
But there was little enthusiasm
for the exercise.

Then began a greater idea
behind all the others
that began with one question only:

And how do you know this?

Daniel started to rise.

Lansing Riot, 2005

The students are again agitated
by the dropping symbol
that coincides so narrowly
with triumphant Spring.

Their hands
are not stained
        with blood,
free of sand
   some barrier
       dissolves

Is it ceremony now?
   Some vestige of Catholicism
arriving with the round-faced Irish
   bad at basketball
       God at agitation.

The tears in their eyes
   contain no emotion
but induced merely
   by a gentle gassing,
just another drug
   pretty in the moonlight
floating high over campus
   dissipating like the past.

In collective oblivion,
   They dance two-step
with blue suits and plastic shields.
Covering several blocks,
it undulates
like a Chinese dragon
whose fiery chant
   bellows only
Que Sera Sera.

A fatherly baton occasionally
    circles through the crowd
to strike a vacancy

as the sacraments
    of struggle
are garments for us all.

And somewhere in the mist
    a lieutenant yawns
beneath his mask
    as he pushes back against
            an inebriated tide.
He is celebrating too.

Emptying the Trash at Orbeca, Inc

November 2002

MEMORANDUM

TO:
NiagaraTech

FROM:
Iowa Health
Systems

Code#2602

RE:
In reference
to your query concerning
employee Helen Kuhn

We all have
good days
and bad days
but for some individuals the highs are higher
and the lows
are lower.

Examples of excessive, expansive behavior
include starting prolonged
extended conversations with strangers
in public,
undertaking actions for which the person
has no experience
or talent
        (e.g. writing a novel, painting, or starting one's own
business)
spending great amounts of money,

indulging in multiple indiscriminate sexual liaisons
often without the aid of birth control.

Speech and thoughts may appear speeded up
and sleep seems less necessary.

###

Process Tracking & Approval-
sign and date for
next
step
in processing...

Tereus in Texas

A broken man steps
   between posturing peasants,
his hawk eyes
   seeking relief in local dives spies
a Procne swallow. Sallow sickly yellow.
A bird of prey, shameless in his suffering,
   left muttering,
"I have within me him who I want."

A chorus greets from seats
   leather broken beats
a country rhythm. They shout, cry, shy
and pose in Ego's shadow.
A favorite haunt for half men,
phony Texans eat breaded strips of Ityeus,
   gobbling, devouring,
and Tereus stuttering,
"I have within me him who I want."

No curious chorus for shame
   the victors, garlanded with spit,
chew on children and childhood.
The buffet a banquet
   and boys know
Tereus will not stomach
   so much insult
as Procne weaves a broken narrative,
   a token affection and loss
still offers a terror and Tereus suffering:
"But I have already eaten,
already eaten,
already eaten,
and I have within me him who I want."

Will the Furies fall upon the chorus,
   their smacking lips and greasy fingers

feign no guilty hand
(though their thumbs point earthward)
    take pleasure in any shame

other than their own
    celebrate deceit and devastation
severed tongues and severed hands
    philomel fucking in the back of a Ford
cowboy style.

    His hollow bones batter
The headlight stars in feathered rage
as evening's children scatter and pray
that they all turn to birds
and they all fly away.

The Muse

She is remarkable
only in her passing
and the strange chemistry
with which she
lingers...
Her face is featureless.
The eyes, the nose, the mouth
blend together into a blank
    silkscreen of flesh
upon which flash expressions
    in brilliant chiaroscuro.

Now she is a toddler
dressed for the season
crying on stage
in seas of red and green.
Sweaty palms pressed
    together
in righteous certainty.

Now she is a puzzling breeze
    the day before a departure
that you might
    still
            feel.

Rarely is she something as grand
as a battered,
 forgotten trophy
    in a vacant room.
And never is she the shining moment of victory,
    never the act. Never the over played moments
of life-fucking.
Not even its undervalued foreplay.

Some special times, she is life's

accidental fondlings.
The stolen smile or
     a coquettish waggling of hips
that presents the strange self-awareness
of one's
inevitable nakedness.

They

They always say
I've heard my father shout
more than once
lips wet with turkey grease.

Always an eager opponent,
Is he as uncomfortable as me,
or the opposite?
As self-satisfied as his rhetoric.

And they are/is
always irrational beady-eyed zealots
dangled before the imagination
of a trigger happy
sleeper, pondering some loss of respect
some insult to one's dignity.

I am with the they
constructing myself out of straw.
First the feet
formed from the dangling epithets
of pundits.
My legs are non-sequiturs.
My waist begs the question.
My chest is split into the
sweet arms of eitherore,
but my mouth is taped shut,
my tongue cut out,
my ears replaced with funnels.

I/They dangle this effigy of absent love.
Burn me.
I was never here.

Throwing Pots

The only leverage
I ever maintained
was perched above the potter's wheel
like Rodin's thinking man.
One hand rests on my chin
speaking no evil beneath my furrowed brow.
The other
drawing from the stubborn mass
any hidden spirit of defiance
as you pinch a pointed argument
of a wasted pitcher.

Judge the asymmetry
of this hollow, earthy vessel in its context.
After all, when a receiver catches a ball
in a field of equally desperate men
is the beauty of his act
measured by yards alone?

So measure my face
burning with the untimely confession
of excusable infidelities,
as a vase collapses
into another ashtray.
I require a Buddha,
Confucius, Jesus maybe
on His better pages
to tease these flowered walls.

Oh, how the clay recognizes
any malicious thought
as I measure your honesty
between my pinched fingers.

If I can not hold a vase
with its slippery form so elusive.

I will return the air to earth again.
Better than bubble wrap,
package organs with my ashtrays.
You nod calmly.
The pitcher balanced perfectly.

Now isn't that nice... Don't you think that's nice.

Even prehistoric man knows
Creation is incomplete without fire
And fire magnifies all imperfections
To a crisis...

The clay, having released
its former self
can affect one last act of will
and self-destruct,
taking with it,
its better crafted cousins.

The Wind, Probably

So that science that was to teach me everything
ends up in a hypothesis, that lucidity founders
in metaphor, that uncertainty is resolved in a
work of art.

— Albert Camus

Aisle Five: Diapers, Baby Goods, Toys, Sanitary Napkins, The Abyss

First memories develop always
    in bleeding colors
of Polaroid desires
shouting at the infant for whom
    the aisles of the grocery store
are the very fields of all there is.

Through the wire mesh of the bass cart,
    through the plastisteel cradle
of commerce,
    he might see
strange skid marks,
like black silly putty
    stretched over white linoleum,
little blemishes of dime store shame
    seeking a diaper.

Or mother's worried brow
    when he points in awe
at so very,
very much
placed for casual consumption.
The beautiful art of the castle
    some other child built
from colored blocks placed
    in moats and portcullises
standing spires,
ordered columns of gargoyle delight.
Now dismantled by a malicious crowd.

It should all go back.

But the mother stops,
    so patient with the howling,

and methodically removes one block
after the other,
so the child can hold it
briefly in his own hands,
and see if it resembles his own pain,
    before settling on
a biscuit!

He unwraps it
    And is still crying
Before the glowing smile
of his mother
who coos happily
    as it's going,
                going,
                        gone!

How Quaint it Has Become

Four suit for Devil's Music on PBS
like the four corners of a square.
Plays like Tiger Woods
long drives on his sax miss the bunkers.
His short game is rare. Where
are we going with this progression
lightly lifted
from Shaman Shostakovich. There
seems to be only a suggestion, passing fare
of my desired witch doctor
who cannot affect oblivion.
The piano sprinkles desktop A-minors
just screensavers that err
on the side, sweet silhouette, of
"Porcine Overture" care
to note the bacon fat on my chest
I squat ape-like on the floor
Tarzan of the T.V.
the bassist is remote controlled
thumbing contrast and tint.
My necktie is knotted around my forehead.
I am hairless like a baby.
Please make a mistake...
the rhythmic cadence fairly trained
beats eggs for quiche
    measures time like a microwave
            Oh God, closes like an oven.
Cultured, Dignified, classical
 and everything it could've been collapses into what I am.

Haiku in Traffic

You tried to kill me
on your way to the suburbs
on I-35.

Angry at the wheel,
our fenders kiss each other
when you flash a gun.

I shrug chrome shoulders
on to San Antonio
afraid to look back.

My car, a gray fish,
having so spawned your anger
still swims gently.

Heritage Park, Corpus Christi

On the park bench at night
I sometimes see
America out of the corner of my eye
dressed in white lace
    walking sheepishly
between the hedge rows.

At least once
she was spotted in the afternoon sun
on the scrolled balconies
overlooking a quinceanera.

And there are stories
that her reflection was
in the sun-tinted silver
of a birthday balloon or
    deep in the background
greasing her lips
on olive-oil ears of roasted corn.

Usually, she dashes about stealthily
    at weddings, a reluctant guest,
unsure if she's been invited,
closing the curtains of picture frame windows
    sorting through the mail of the dead
and trying to ignore
the ceaseless grumbling
        of the ocean.

Texas Beckons

The reluctant docent
explains the awkward birth.
How it moved
in pieces around the Nueces Valley.
Originally Spanish, La Espana.
She insists,
Watch the film, really
the video can explain it better.
And we're off...

Into the courtyard, playing catch
into the battlefield, miming soldiers
into the chapel, feigning Catholic.
All the way, artifacts breathing orders.
A broken bell, a broken lance head, broken
Earthenware, musketballs, axe handles
Snuff jars, borders broken, broken Spanish
In the casements,
Broken plates, cups, crutches
So many and like the walls
Pieced together with meticulous care

The presidio rises on the Texas bluff
A jig saw fortress.
The world has not known such fragile walls.
A curator tosses me a plate
Look, Mira!

I trace the gluey tracks with my fingers
It is still a plate, cross your eyes
Chuckling, he passes.
I cross my eyes,
The landscape stretches before me
in Monet shadows, rough
and irregular
when you touch it.

Detritus of the Dead at Presidio La Bahia

The long dead leave no mess
   no bottle caps, no cigarette butts
   no tissues, socks, no empty bottles
only us,
   scattered over their tidy courtyard,
schlepping champagne bottles
   along these after hours ramparts,
casing the easements of graves. At best
        we are
well-intentioned intruders
of a world preserved from us
   in plastic window cupboards,
longing to be the broken lance head,
   longing to be the pottery comb.
Or at least to know
the mystery behind
asking fragments
(unknown 13-unknown 42A)
 who could tell us
the difference between six hundred
and three thousand.

The dead have their exclamation point
   and cannot understand our anxious queries
in the barracks
   in the towers
by the well whisperings in the church.
So that when we return
   drunk to the officer's quarters,
the long forgotten manifest in swamp gas,
   circle the air in otherworldly orbs of light
channel their contented voices
        from deep south slumbering
and wish for us,
   in our bleary-eyed credulous dreamings
to rest in peace.

Railroad Rapture

I saw it first
   through the windows of the Capitol Limited
where the tracks hug wintry Michigan.
My feet could not even touch the carpet.
The steward,
   stocky and dark,
The steward,
   all Coca-Cola,
Reserved the cans for the adults,
   biting me to the core
with his plastic cups.

My mother abandoned my defense
for the dining car.
Yet, there it was.
Sun-setting Indiana
   centered on the burned out trunk
of a fallen oak.
I drifted past the steward
up through the shaky rivets
   of the sleeper.
Quickly, wispy,
   I was white clouds.
   I was white contrails.
Slowly I descended beneath the rusty bridge
   and stole myself.
Above the mossy grass,
   I lingered to kiss
the broken trees,
   scrubbing between the roots and refuse
past bottle caps and fireflies
and up again
   to the bridge, the cars
through an accountant's window
   and forward through narrow lanes
so that when she returned
I had already,

slowly,
          condensed
back into my seat.

Tagging the Blackboard

There is no thesis statement
        to "West Side Bitches!"
even in the students guilt grinning
at the middle finger of the dotted eye.

There is no thesis statement
        to "West Side Bitches!"
even in its antinomial font
except to shout the collective we
to pander audacity to amused poverty,
        red-eyed from not blinking.

There is no thesis statement
        scrawled on overpasses,
making claim to the view,
none in garbage bins
        with cliché comments
on the nature of refuse,
none touring distant lands on freight cars
        that might make new
where I've already been.
There are only
        these chicken scratch furies,
long lettered and lessonless.

Not even, anymore
the elegantly sprayed silver and blue,
letters like angelic bubbles,
rising from the social conscious seventies
high above the railroad rust,
        above the wintry steamvents
the burnt out frames of abandoned cars.

Not even a comma
        to give my students
some direction:
        WEST SIDE,

BITCHES!

I've never seen it
    in a church,
never on so nice a day
never has someone slammed shut,
    with such ferocity,
the only open window.

En Soi

I

The glove appears
in the slushy afterbirth of winter.
The knitting on the forefinger
unstitched a wooly foreskin
that agonizes its predecessor.
Still it sits
floating, waves
from a center of neglect
at the occasional passerby.

II

The glove has personality.
Just earlier today
in a parking lot
behind the mall
it illustrated a point
about Sartre.
Many agreed
the glove
displayed a most subtle insight.
Still others felt it was a poor analogy.
The glove weeps.

III

I can no longer abide the glove.
My patience is exhausted.
It thinks now that it is a rock star
and that the flakes in its
four-fingered dreadlocks
are bits of dandruff

that it might easily shake off.
It has grown contemptuous
manifest
in the occasional extended finger.
The glove rages.

IV

A steel grey sky descends ominously
upon a forgetful ragged glove
that has become well known
in the shopping mall parking lot.
It hallucinates like a drug addict
that can neither remember
nor forget.
It contains no malice toward
the falling snow,
but waits with a Hindu's patience.
The glove is.

V

A man trespasses on a dream
arguing politics with
the most agreeable opposition
who nods eagerly in affirmation.
The snow drifts
crouch like colorless
revolutionaries
and the ice beneath his feet
seems endless.
The glove is no more.

Inaugural Sun

A Stone-faced African swallow
shuffles and dips
his plastic maw
to gather the sky
in tablespoons.

A patriot's panting
manifest eddies
in January vapors
    only grudgingly
disappears.
A moment's hesitation before
    the coronal podium
exposes an awkward hope.
Will his speech
    the family exonerate?
Will he damn the sodomites
    In sentences punctuated with freedom?
An ownership(freedom) society is our manifest(freedom)
destiny
    And who owns (freedom) me?

No thanks or applause
from the vacant anticipation
in the idle rows of fold-out chairs
but as luck would have it

He spies Jefferson
    embossed in nickel
staring back from an icy tomb.
His features marred
    by untimely gravel
His hair is bubblegum algae.

To the disappointed
    he offers what relief he may.

Inside

I often find base boards
stained with whispering words
    drip-
     ping
and incredulous,
when letters slip free
from the cracked grouting,
pushed along
by the gentle shuffling of human feet.

Surprised and joyous at their own coherence,
they run everywhere.
Occasionally I might pinch one
from between the fibers of a shag carpet,
or be shocked when the words crawl restlessly
down drainpipes,
or nest peacefully in an underwear bin.

More than a few escape, I know,
through the sub-flooring
down the termite funnels
until they drift flake-like
onto the unfamiliar texture of soil.

Jazz Appreciation

Some call it
a passing gas
the trombones break wind
in their low guttural syncopation
and our love
sublimated joy for an audacious song
that should be titled
"The Inappropriate Guest"

Others call it
the rocking motion of sex
the trumpet an extended phallus
urging us to climax
to the siren's call of "Bakhtin's Wheel"
as the saxophone
provides a surprising suction sound

Or does it contain
a world of suffering and the song
is only and always "Middle Passage"

Listen again...
It is the player's part after all
and he waits for the beauty
that is undigested genius.
The song is titled "Whose?"
Once stated, it lingers long lost
in the listener
waiting patiently for someone
hoping someone will claim ownership of it.

Understanding Picasso

Pablo collects pebbles.
Mounds of them
and processes
splitting those from mere rocks
rigid standards
that stones must acquiesce to.

Has it been skipped along stagnant pools
or cast forward from the center of the earth
to be cooled and polished under glorious sun.
Does it speak?
Some have been cut by rain into
six carat granite displacing hollow time
and are mere stones no more but epic,
leaving Pablo to reflect sadly that
the destiny of men lies in rocks.

Reminding Patience
Slighting Courage
Pablo spreads these before him
On the breezeway and over the garden
Terra Firma Earth Quarry
For Pablo will not walk on pebbles
of broken glass
but only on the very tears of God.
Everything is real
with eyes open and pure
a melancholy man already pale
under September blue
is spanked by sunlight
and adds the proper shading.

Posting Elaine

Brazilian Beauty
seeks happy American home
enjoys cowboys, movies, and
all things American. Speak English.

I

He reluctantly tells the story
of their courtship
in a fashion most concise.
I.N.S does not stand for InterNational Suitor (she weeps
when she cries).

The details mask
a guilty exchange
for the story
has no
butterflies, serendipitous encounters, weeping laughter,
serenade, sweaty midnight quarrels…

neurotic withdrawal. (shouts when she is
                                            angry).

The picture:
Golden skin and a practiced smile,
arms placed delicately
to hide a tattoo left open
by a flower pattern dress.
She is present.
She looks like cologne.

Gone is the crooked smile
of his youth.
He has swollen now…
his body accustomed to
a practiced lethargy

seeks the great efficiency of motion.

Now he can only accuse:
Were we not gray
at the temples?
Was it ever any different?

    II

He bought a lamp on the internet
When we started college.

                    Justamente com seus pais

An eagle rising victory lamp…
Gold plate over silver plate.

                    Elaine Pallone e Trevor
                    Montgomery Monroe

Avian feathers spread open
into a perfect V
touch the soft light

              convidiam para a cerimonia
              religiosa de seu casamento

the noble head arched upwards
hoping to see the holy sun,

              a realixar – se as onze horas
do dia vinte de setembro
de dois mil e tres

an engraving of the artist
etched on the base.

na Capela do Educandario Santo Antonio

he keeps it still

Os noivas receberao os convidados no
Clube dos Inglesas, Boa Vista

Beside a Persian alarm clock and a ceramic frog.

You Are Not Prickly Hamlet

You are not prickly Hamlet
    having Polonius killed
only to sit with tortured double entendres
while cleverly investigating me.

But lie panting an Elizabethan smile
    crusty blood lines paws and jaws
Morning eyes gleam proud as you tap out
in heavy breath
the more dramatic moments of your watch.

The victim is artistically rendered
    The lengthy tail circled about the abdomen
to touch the incisors and snout.
    The crimson pool mirrors its symmetry
and you too,
so high above it.

A mockery of your sanguine pose,
    tail wagging as if to lesson:
No thought should cloud the determined spirit.
    Having put itself between me and you,
now the intrepid rat lies blood and fur.
    Deed done, to the courtyard I shall retire.

And with imperfect gait, you lumber past
        four legged self assurance
leaving me and my morning coffee
wounded with doubt.

Melting Prometheus

White torso of snow
scraped from the parking lot
with an awkward garden shovel.
The tradition of the
three ball format
proving illusory.
My baby brother's dream
of cartoons withdrawn
amidst the reality of Texas snow.

A wig
we have for hair
and that won't melt,
and neither will the olive eyes
or the burgundy scarf.

A Caucasian child,
two feet four inches,
weighing around twenty pounds,
blonde hair,
black eyes,
wearing a burgundy scarf,
created from the sky.

Stares through pimento pits
in pensive wonder
eroding his inclimate judgments
onto the idol worshippers
of the passing.

Still standing with me
after the rest of the snow has melted.
The nose is flatter.
The heels are gone.
One of the olives has dropped below the other.
No more chin.

Then he is on his side.
The pale skin losing its color
in little rivulets.
My baby brother is afraid.
He won't talk to it
or go near it.

He's gone.
I pick up the wig,
put it on.
The scarf, too.
Block out the sun
with rotting black eyes.
Nothing left but this cold, puddle of water.

Lover's Quarrel at the State Fair, 2010

Your conspicuous widow black
   shadows a pastel Monet
   of red and orange
and a Fair's urgency.

From the distance of South Texas,
   it made enough sense to arrive
as two pilgrims might. Here, it's all you,
            misplaced.

Some pass you to the ring toss.
   Some jostle you helpless
on the move to the Ferris Wheel.
Most fear you as the witch
   of the petting zoo
and drowned you in a sea
upon which
   you cannot float
high enough
   to survey my love...

or you're burning,
swaying to and fro,
   flickering red then orange
then red again,
   as they battle on their consumptive quest
for some different brew:
Deep-fried beer, beer on a stick, Beer-B-Q.

I remain a victim
of the crowd's inconsiderate
undertow
deceiving me into my solitary past
separating us so that
by the gated shore you're left stranded.
Teary-eyed like a repentant sinner
   reluctantly baptized

by the waters of commerce,
exhausted, you absent-mindedly kneel
    as if awaiting the blessing and benediction
of Big Tex.

Anything of Substance Creates Shadow

and this picture has been painted before.
The pear is shaped like a woman
amazingly dry between two apples
and a metaphor.

In an incidental bowl
carved from live oak
by a machine
the grapes do not
get to touch her
spill over onto grassy marble
looked down upon by four gored oranges
opaque under the fluorescent glow.

Centering the centerpiece
is an almost waxy cliché
but more than that somehow
the deceptive spine
green and calloused with pastels,

twists and turns back on itself
through the sweeter meat of
the shoulders down through
fleshy thighs and the flower.

The stem is brown
reaching for yellow.

Stocking the Nursery

Prayers suggest a kind of hope
   long abandoned in my late,
      anxious twenties
when Pandora serenaded beer stein microphones
and I was content to leave the box under the tree
   or regift.

We believed
   but ceased daring anymore,
so diapers were bought economy size,
   not as prayers,
with each bubbled butt an "our father."
   No…

Between the crib, the changer, dragon mobiles, and onesies,
with soothies, pacifiers, comfort quilts, and night lights,
among bottle brushes, aspirators, booties, rattles,
Pandora was playing the dice
every damn day, in fear and trembling
of every seven. Not me.

Honestly, I was buying litter
for Shrödinger's cat.
Equations like fasteners connecting
   the soiled earth
above which you drift in a balloon
   of probabilities. One in ten thousand…
One in five thousand…
One in five, one in two, one.

Until the doctor's routine peek,
objective speculation of the you there,
   or not there.
So your head emerges
photon-like from the slot
   and waves condense
into the particles

of your black diamond gaze.

Only then can I box my past
    of ossified cats.
Seal it tight with your mother,
    and sit finally
at the threshold
    of this new reality.

www.ingramcontent.com/pod-product-compliance
Lightning Source LLC
Chambersburg PA
CBHW032027090426
42741CB00006B/760